Split The Fairway

The Golfer's Guide to Increasing Distance, Reducing Back Pain and Playing the Golf That Makes Your Friends Jealous

By Dr. Josh Satterlee

First Edition

Printed in the United States of America

ISBN 13: 978-1519446060

Table of Contents

Introduction

I originally went to college to study engineering. But during my sophomore year I was walking through the Portland airport on an athletics trip and I heard, "Josh Satterlee, please pick up a white courtesy phone." Let me tell you, there wasn't good news on the other end. My father had been diagnosed with brain cancer.

I took a year off from school in order to take care of my father. He was a big golfer, and early on in his disease, we were able to play a few rounds together. Even as he got worse, we would sometimes go for an evening drive through his home course—Wood Ranch Golf Club in Simi Valley, California—in a golf cart.

My father was in a lot of pain. One thing that stuck out to me through his health-care odyssey is that his chiropractor was the only physician that tried to eliminate the pain without the use of drugs or surgery. The others prescribed meds, meds and more meds. It got to the point where the law of diminishing returns applied. Many times, my dad refused the pain killers because he said they made him too foggy. He chose pain over being in a stupor and not remembering the last few months of his life.

When I returned to college, this experience with my father led me to pursue a degree in health so that I could go to chiropractic college. I had witnessed the amazing change that can occur in bodies in real time. With chiropractic, it isn't, "Hey, take this drug and in four to six weeks you should feel better." Instead it's you walk in today and you leave moving and feeling better. I thought that was very powerful.

Now, the way I got involved in golf was by way of family. My maternal grandfather was actually a professional, and he taught some pretty famous people, including boxer Joe Louis; Johnny Weissmuller, the Olympic swimmer who played Tarzan on the original TV show; and Billie Jean King, tennis star.

Third from left Johnny Weissmuller.

Fifth from left my grandfather, Earl Martin.

My grandfather, Earl Martin, third from left.
Bob Hope fifth from left.

Snead Goes Long Route to Win

Sam Snead and my grandfather.
Snead beat him but it took 23 holes.

So, you could say that golf runs in my blood.

My dad learned, then I learned, and we fell in love with the game. The first nine-hole round of golf I ever played was at the age of 6. The first full 18 was at the age of 14. I could go on and on about golf. Some of my fondest memories were spending time with my dad and acting as his caddie. He and I would spend mornings out on the course, and I would have a great time hearing all the stories and observing how he and his buddies swung their clubs.

Many years later, I injured my back while playing a round. It was the return of a college injury I had suffered while doing competitive Olympic-style weightlifting. I felt the same pain all over again, but I decided to play through it. I took the next swing and my back hurt worse. It was almost debilitating, but I was on the 13th hole, so it was easier to go forward than back.

I decided to swing again.

I noticed two other things:

1) That I could not get any distance whatsoever.

2) I was slicing the purple hell out of the ball.

So, the ball was going nowhere and I was in pain. I wanted to figure out why that was. I had an understanding of the body, and yet I couldn't figure out this golf swing problem.

Soon after, I began to study with the Titleist Performance Institute (TPI), which is the human performance lab started by Titleist to find out how to get people to be better at golf and give them the ability to play more rounds per month.

Titleist owns more than 50 percent of the golf ball market. It needs people to buy more golf balls, and people only buy more balls once they lose the golf balls they already own. Golfers don't lose golf balls when they are sitting at home with a sore back.

Through working with TPI, studying its research and findings and using the data, I found out how to straighten out my shot and how to make my back feel better.

Just understanding how my body moved during the swing helped a lot. Ironically, I ended up changing to a very upright swing, just like my dear old dad's. I had previously followed my brother's style, which was more athletic and "squatty" (similar to Charley Hoffman's style).

Through TPI, I also realized that many golfers were struggling with the same troubles I had but weren't able to do much about it. The TPI program offers a very exact body of knowledge that includes specific treatments, exercises and stretches that can change your game.

I began bringing golfers into my practice as patients and have been working with golfers ever since. I have had the pleasure of adding yardage to many a golfer's game, including 37 yards to a man who was then 63 years old. Talk about a happy guy! He had been playing golf for 45 years, and this transformation only took us two months.

On the other end of the age spectrum, I have also had the pleasure of helping juniors create distance. One of my patients was a High School Sophmore. She tried out for the golf team as a freshman but didn't make the cut. With my help she added 11 yards, qualified as a Sophmore and became their #3 player.

The statistic that most sums up my success with helping golfers is this: I have helped 24 players who had gotten to the point where they could only play one round a week, if that, because their backs caused them so much pain. Every single one of those 24 individuals is now playing three times a week with no back pain.

I am proudest of this type of success because these people were unable to do more of something they love. This kind of win is what I live for.

I believe we need to share this method with the world. How many golfers are out there who are being limited by their physical abilities and not their skills?

I know how bad it is to be out there with a back that's hurting. Your round runs twice as long and you can't get the ball anywhere. It sucks.

I have been a chiropractor for nine years now, and I have been studying with the Titleist Performance Institute for seven of them.

This has proven to be a very rewarding combination. I hope you will keep reading to learn how it might help you, too.

This book is broken up into sections. It goes in the order I usually follow when patients come into my office. Many of them are golfers and they not only want me to help them get out of pain, but to reap the benefits of our gym, Anthem Fitness, where we offer the performance program.

When a golfer comes in, our first priority is to get them "durable," which means building a base level of strength and flexibility. Once that is established, we crank up the training to create massive distance. That speed and power training is the third aspect of our program.

Chapter One: Limiters to Your Golf Game—Money, Time and Lower Back Pain

Back in 1996, Titleist knew two things:

1) It owned more than half of the golf-ball market.

2) Its business expansion relied on getting more golfers to lose more golf balls.

To get you to lose more golf balls, Titleist decided to figure out how to get you to play more rounds. It surveyed players, namely the recreational variety, asking questions like, "What holds you back from playing more golf?"

Among the resulting reasons, what surprised me most was that "lack of improvement" wasn't even in the top 10. People didn't care about that. They will put up with a lot of bad golf before they quit.

The big limiters were:

1) Time. A round of golf took too much time out of the day or week. For the working golfer this is a big barrier.

2) Money. It cost too much. I think we can all agree that this is an expensive sport.

3) Low back pain.

From my perspective, I can't help you get more time and I can't provide you with more money or more affordable golf, but low back pain is an easily fixed problem.

By asking the right questions and focusing on the right tests, it's a solvable problem.

If your goal is to play more golf, there's a good chance that low back pain is one of the things that keeps you from doing that. Certainly, in my patient population, that absolutely used to be true. Their backs were limiting them from playing more rounds.

But here is the crazy thing: If you are a guy of around 55 or 60 who has been playing for years, then you have never been more experienced at golf than you are today. You have never read so much or played as many rounds as you have today, and you have never understood the game as well.

So why aren't you getting better?

You know more, your course management is great, your mental capacity is higher, you know what shots to take and which ones not to and there is a good chance you have played the course you are playing quite a few times before.

So why aren't you getting better?

We want to identify the reason. It usually comes down to your body. Your physical abilities are not nearly as good as your golf skills. So if we look at your handicap, whatever your index is, it's really a combination of how skilled you are and what your body can actually produce.

If you were 25 years old but had the same knowledge you have today, you probably would be one hell of a golfer. Your understanding of slope, your course management skills, and your smarts about shot selection are so much further ahead today.

But when you were 25, you didn't have as much knowledge as you have today, and today you don't have the body of a 25 year old.

So, what we really want to do is get the answer to the question, "What's holding you back from moving like a 25-year-old?"

Your handicap is actually lower than what the number says right now. If fact, my bet is that if you can just move and be flexible and strong, your handicap would be probably half of what it is now.

The number-one limiter of that strength and flexibility is lower back pain. Actually, there are actually other things limiting you, but lower back pain is the red flag, the sign we see that says, "Hey, this person is really screwed up."

How many incredibly skilled golfers are playing one time a week or even less, struggling through and thinking to themselves, "Man, I'm getting worse! I don't even know if I want to show up tomorrow"?

Imagine if you could work on something for two or three months and then go out there, with your buddies all betting against you, and hit a drive 25 yards farther than you usually hit it. You'd clean up. How good would that feel?

Just picture it – you're sitting there at the grill with everybody pushing their money towards you. You wind up looking like you have a haystack of money in front of you – how incredible would that feel?

That's why you play the game. Not to just sit there and struggle. So let's help you feel that way.

Pain and Distance

Keep in mind that "low back pain" is the common term, but what I see with a lot of people is it's another way of saying "crappy distance." When your back is really hurting, you cannot produce good distance. I see guys that used to drive the ball 260-280 yards now barely reaching 200. It's embarrassing, and it makes that round so damn long. When you have a 500-yard par-5, you have got to get two shots in to even to see the flag, for goodness sakes.

There are two groups of people I see that have lower back pain in golf. The first are those who feel pain in the lower back and it slows down their swing. Slower swing equals less distance. You're certainly not going to be taking the shots that require a lot movement on the ball because it's become harder to hit those.

Your body just doesn't want to move in that way anymore. Those people start their swing with pain, they feel pain during the round and afterward they're in pain.

There is a whole other group of people who have physical issues (related to lower back, tight hips or other restrictions, which we'll cover later) and they don't even know it, but when we have them get a 3-D Analysis to see how they move, they are actually slowing down their swing to avoid feeling pain.

Their body inherently knows that you swing this fast or in that direction, there will be pain, so it won't let you. Therefore, it is not going to swing that fast because it doesn't want to feel pain. When we ask them, "Hey, do you have lower back pain?"

Their answer is often, "No."

As they're about to find out through proper diagnosis, the actual answer is that they are physically compromised but have a bad swing that never gets to the point where it is fast enough to produce lower back pain.

The body knows it has a weakness and therefore protects itself. If you were a pitcher throwing a fastball and your body recognizes that every time you throw over 98 miles an hour you have shoulder pain, it caps your speed below that. Then you throw 96 and I ask if your shoulder hurts. It doesn't, but you are not producing the heat like you used to.

In golf, pain or no pain, if you aren't driving long and well it still might mean there's something going on in your back or in your body that needs to be addressed, because at some point you will wind up reducing your swing speed. Pretty soon your friends will laugh at you and tell you to move up to the next tee box. Even worse, you might agree with them.

When we get a decrease in low back pain, almost 100 percent of the time we see distance increase by a large margin, which is incredibly rewarding. Yes, it's great to sit in the clubhouse with no pain in your back, but it's even better to win the round and say, "Who wants to take me on tomorrow?"

The reason your back hurts is probably the same reason why you can't move as well as you used to. There are movement limitations—your hamstrings are tight, or your ankles are not flexible anymore, etc. Those things rob you of consistency as well as distance.

The only thing worse than a short and consistent shot is a short and inconsistent shot. It's the hang-ups and bang-ups and the tightness in different places that makes it more difficult to hit the same shot over and over, and that really makes golf tough.

A great approach to improving your game is to first help you move in a way that is consistent and allows you to hit the same shot, even if it is a little shorter than you want it to be. From there we build into a shot that's both consistent and long.

There are a lot of reasons that makes this a winning approach. Ninety-nine percent of the people I see stretching are doing the wrong stretches, or worse, they're doing ones that will cause them to be in more pain. They are addressing certain areas that might feel tight, but not the areas that produce great golf play.

We are going to cover all of these things, including my favorite golf stretches, in later chapters.

Are You Going to Try to Change My Swing Style?

One thing I want to make clear is that we are not interested in your swing style. I don't care if you swing like John Daly or Jim Furyk. The mechanics of your swing must be sound no matter whose swing you are trying to emulate.

I don't care if you are a stack-and-tilt guy or you're from the Leadbetter school or you're a dual plane guy—it doesn't matter. But there are certain mechanics that have to be in place for you to apply your skill successfully and not have pain.

I have had the pleasure of working with some of the best swing coaches in the world, and I've been able to see which ones really understand the body. I've also had conversations with the swing coaches of all of our high end players. We also work closely with the Butch Harmon School, which is the number-one school in golf and is only about a mile from my office.

Chapter 2: Common Swing Faults

The Titleist Performance Institute has identified the twelve most common swing faults or swing characteristics. You may recognize some of these in yourself or in other golfers.

A lot of people call swing faults by different names. I have included diagrams of each of them so that you can see what they are and be able to tell if you have been told you have one or more of them by a different name.

S-Posture

Correct

S-posture

C-Posture

Correct

C-posture

Loss of Posture

Correct

Loss of Posture

Flat Shoulder Plane

Correct

Flat Shoulder Plane

Early Extension

Correct Early Extension

Over the Top

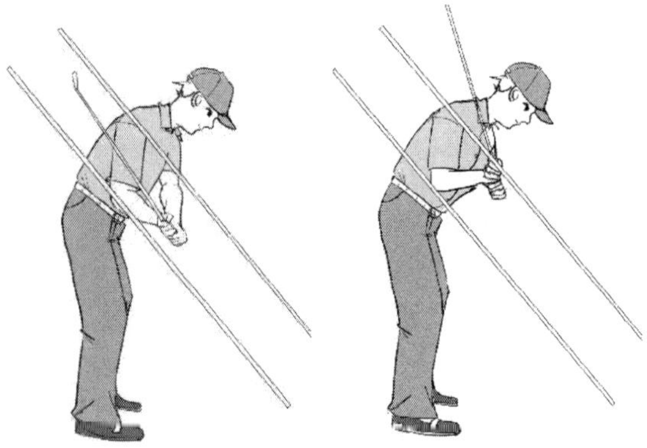

Correct Over the Top

Sway

Correct

Sway

Slide

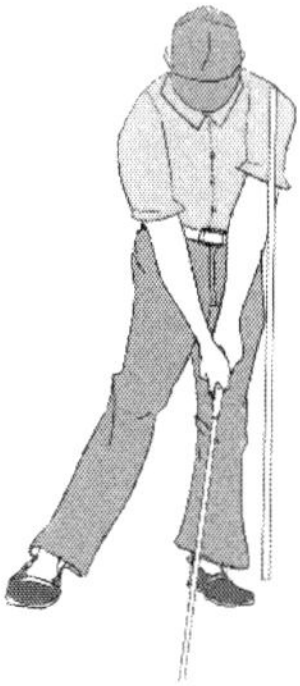

Correct

Slide

Reverse Spine Angle

Correct Reverse Spine Angle

Hanging Back

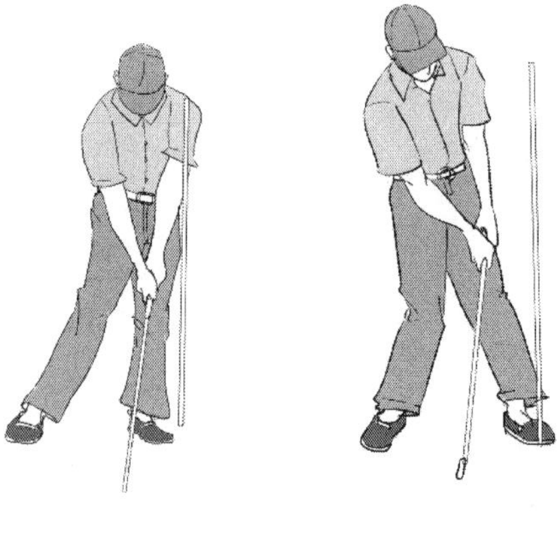

Correct Hanging Back

Casting or Early Release

Correct

Casting/Early Release

Chicken Winging

Correct

Chicken Winging

Now, what does that all mean? Every player may have one or more of these faults. Some players have none, and we typically call those guys professionals. But even some professionals have swing faults. What we know for certain is that there are certain physical findings that produce each one of those faults.

I'll hear someone say, "Oh yeah, I am hanging back," and then they go over the swing drills that they are using to reduce that problem.

But what they are not doing is reducing the physical issues that are causing them to have that swing fault in the first place.

There may be limitations such as a weak core, tight hamstrings and bad balance that cause all those things to occur.

The reason I bring it up is that we can directly correlate what we see in your golf swing with what is wrong with your body. Some of these swing faults are highly correlated with lower back pain. In fact, there is one that guarantees back pain.

At some point, anyone with this swing fault will create lower back pain, just because it loads the anatomy in a certain way that will eventually result in pain. If you want to be in pain and not hit the ball anywhere, adopt this posture.

Look again at the swing-fault diagrams and see if you can identify it. Don't read the next sentence until you do.

So, what is your answer? The swing fault that causes pain 100 percent of the time is reverse spine angle. Your head and spine lean toward your target instead of leaning away.

This really crunches the tiny joint ligaments and facet joints on the lead side (the left side of your body if you're right-handed), so when you rip into the ball, that crunching happens at a high speed. This will lead to some very serious problems, such as blowing a disc.

The most famous player who has this swing fault is Colin Montgomery. So if you want to see what this looks like, check out his swing.

The Shortest Hitters

At my clinic we examine what the TPI calls the "body-swing connection" because it helps us identify how we can best improve your swing. If we intelligently identify the right things and improve your body, we know your swing will improve.

Short hitters have very common correlations, perhaps the most common thing being that they do not use their hips to turn and create power. Rather, they use the muscles of their lower back to create the turn and power.

Well, the problem with that is the muscles in the low back aren't very big. They are not designed for that kind of power. Plus, the joints in your low back aren't designed for powerful rotation—unlike the hip joints, which flourish with rotation.

The low back is designed to support you, or to act as a transmission. When you turn that transmission into an engine, it will fail. This is a common cause of lower back pain.

The short hitters of the world come in with backs that are in a lot of pain and are really tired, because those muscles are overworked.

The shortest hitters also move like a log. They don't create any X-factor or "disassociation" in their body. Basically we want you to develop the ability for your hips to point one way and for your shoulders to point the other.

With short hitters, their hips and shoulders stay locked together. They don't get the club head speed they need. There's nowhere to develop power and speed because you've got to have length of swing.

If the equation for speed is Distance x Acceleration, and we reduce the distance (by a lot), then there is nowhere to accelerate. Therefore, you can never develop enough speed and you're back at an embarrassingly short driving distance. The longer your swing, the more time you have to create power and speed.

With the right treatment, the right diagnosis and some specific rehab exercises we have developed, these faults can be corrected.

But It Feels So Right!

These swing faults are there because they feel right to you when you swing. It feels to you like that's how you should swing. This is because there is some other thing wrong with your body — unknown to you. You don't realize how bad you are until you get on film or 3-D.

Often my patients then say, "That's not me!" They are very disappointed to realize that the picture I took actually is them.

The guy whose shoulders and hips are locked together swings that way because to swing otherwise doesn't feel right. He can't even sense that he is moving and swinging like a robot.

When the big limiter is discovered and corrected, the swing changes. Then the new swing will feel right. In fact, I'll sometimes have players imitate their old swing to demonstrate how bad it was.

When I ask, "Would ever want to go back?" the answer is always a resounding "No way!"

That's when I know we have cured a golfer's "subconscious dysfunction."

It actually took me awhile to understand how to create change in my players. Even if you know the solution, sometimes it's hard to get the player to realize what they are doing wrong. And a lot of players who do understand what they are doing wrong often don't realize why they are doing it wrong.

A few years ago I was lucky enough to have a mentor make sense of all of this. In fact, he also illustrated that the learning doesn't stop when a player "knows" what to do. He must go further than that, to where that knowledge is subconscious.

There are actually four stages to learning a new swing, or any new motion that we are trying to correct or teach. It doesn't matter if it's teaching golf or how to throw a fastball or how to turn snow skis. Everyone goes through the same stages. We use this in our rehab process, too, because so many people need to truly learn how to move to avoid getting re-injured. If you stop too early and fail to get to the fourth stage then you will most likely return to your old habits and therefore return to pain.

These four stages are:

1) **Subconscious Dysfunction.** We take you through our process and analysis. You didn't know what was wrong (it was subconscious), and we know it wasn't working (dysfunction). When we perform the correct tests at this stage, it gets us to …

2) **Conscious Dysfunction.** You're now aware of what you're doing incorrectly. And even though you may know it very well, it is still dysfunctional. The most important step here is to discover what exactly is wrong with the body and to demonstrate it as true to you in order to begin correcting it. This stage is often uncomfortable because you now recognize your bad habit all the time—like when a friend highlights how many times you use a certain word in speaking. Awareness helps us move past it and on to the next stage.

3) **Conscious Function.** At this stage, if you think about it, you can do the right thing swing-wise. You know that you need to do particular stretches, ones that will allow you to turn more, for instance. You now know what feeling you must create in your body to produce the move you really want. One problem remains: You don't have time to really think about such things during the swing. If you have

to think about every single step, your swing will be clunky and rough, and we are after smooth.

4) **Subconscious Function.** This is where the magic happens. It's tough to get to this stage, and most people bail out once they know what to feel. However, to have long-term success, you must be able to move and perform in a subconscious manner, never having to think about it. Just like throwing a ball. When you learn the best method and it sinks in, you don't have to give it any thought. You perform a coordinated, fast, smooth, synchronous movement.

A Game of Options

Again, I am not a swing coach. My job is not to tell you what style of swing works best for you, nor how you should hit the ball or where the ball should be in your stance or anything like that. I want to develop a game of options for you. Here's what I mean by that.

When the best players in the world pull out a single club, say a 6-iron, they have multiple options. At the minimum they have nine options, high, low and medium, fade straight or draw. And you can have a high draw, a low draw or a mid draw, which amounts to nine options. There could be more: You could punch it, you could keep it low under the wind, or you could really get that thing up high to bite the green.

The worst players in the world are the less experienced players who don't have options. They pull out a 6-iron and they hope to all that's holy that they connect. They are certainly not going to be able pick where it lands or at what angle it comes in.

So when we look at your body we want you to have the option of moving. We don't want you to have to swing in a certain way because you're being forced to due to tightness or lack of strength or anything like that. We want you to be able to play any shot you want and move any way you want with absolutely no risk.

After we get you moving, that's probably the best time to work with your swing coach because you'll have better ability to move and they can shape a perfect swing for you. We even suggest that you bring your swing coach with you, if you have one. In fact, we enjoy playing a game called "Guess Your Swing," where after the evaluation, we ask the swing instructor, "Does this player swing this way, or make this move?" We aren't really guessing here; we know that there is only a certain way the player can swing based on their restrictions and movements.

Chapter Three: How Hidden Body Issues Rob You of Distance

The three most important areas of the body when it comes to movement restrictions are your hips, lower back and thoracic spine. We'll cover all three of these in detail, but let me start by talking about the hips.

Hips

The hip, if you remember from anatomy class, is just a big, huge ball-and-socket joint.

It's an incredible joint with a very big strong bony structure. Mechanically it's very strong, thanks in part to being surrounded by huge muscles called glutes, plus a few others.

That means if we look at the body, the hips should be producing your power not just in golf but in any sport (except maybe swimming). Just look at sprinters: They have huge hips and enormous glute muscles. Boxers, quarterbacks and anybody who is producing power has to have big glutes because that is the pelvic powerhouse of the body. The hips are the source of all that energy.

What we see in most recreational golfers is that they don't use their hips for power. Instead they overuse their lower back. We talked about this in Chapter Two as the consistent trait in short hitters. I'm sure you've played with someone who has no noticeable glutes and just cannot hit the ball anywhere.

If the goal is to be a long hitter, I can tell you right now, your time and money are best spent in addressing your hips. They need to move in six different ranges of motion: forward, which we call flexion; backwards, which we call extension; rotate in and out, also known as internal and external rotation; and across your body and away from your body, or adduction and abduction.

Combined, those motions produce that smooth, consistent swing we see that professional players have.

When your hips are tight or weak, you can't swing the way you need to, and that's when we see this jerky, log-roll-type swing. When your hips are tight or weak, you might be the guy who chunks out a divot or misses the ball completely.

So the hips are really the centerpiece of how you move. It's where most of your power comes from, and it's how you develop a smooth, consistent swing.

Out of those six motions in the hips, the one that's most commonly missing is what we call internal rotation, especially on your lead hip. If you're a right-handed golfer this would be your left hip.

If you can't rotate into that lead hip, oftentimes you will lift up and create at least one of those swing faults. We are going to see flat shoulder play, a loss of posture, early extension, etc. Those things create a lack of distance and a bad round.

People often tell me, "My lower back is sore from golf." Or "I try to stretch my lower back all the time." I want to ask them, "Why are you banging your head against the wall? If you've been trying to stretch your low back for three years and it's not changing, why is that?" Well, the real issue is that your hips don't move enough, and that's what we need to fix.

Keep in mind this also means that all the stretches you are doing are the wrong stretches. You can stretch for 20 minutes, but if you are stretching the wrong thing, it's not going to make you feel better or hit the ball any better. So, let's make sure we are targeting the right thing.

Yes, some stretches for golf are often difficult and take a lot of effort, but if you put in about five minutes a day, you will soon notice a change in your golf swing. I've had patients stretch their hip and then tell me they added 15 yards to their drive.

When your hips don't move, it forces your low back to move too much and actually a lot of the swing problems that people have is due to a tight lower back. That's your body reacting by trying to tense up your low back to save itself. It's not that your lower back is the problem. Your low back is probably getting way overused, trying to do the work your hips should be doing. You're beating the crap out of it.

Whereas if you stretch out your hips and get them to do the work, your lower back will feel a lot better because it doesn't have to do so much work.

The Trained Monkey

I like to share a little story with my patients to illustrate a point. I'll share it here with you.

A friend of mine was walking through Thailand and he said there was a monkey on one of the streets. You could pay the monkey 25 cents and then you point to an area of your body and the monkey would rub that area for you for about five minutes. Pay the monkey a quarter and point at your shoulder and the monkey will rub your shoulder. It seems like a good idea, right?

The problem is that I see a lot people going to other chiropractors, physical therapists and other doctors and they get a trained monkey. They say, "My low back hurts," and the doctor looks at the low back or X-rays of the low back or does an injection on the low back or applies ultrasound to the lower back.

This is despite the fact that the lower back is not typically the problem. It's the site of the pain but not the source of the problem.

Same with golfers. The lower back is very likely not the issue. By way of example, it is possible that your hips don't work and when your hips don't work, your lower back tries to compensate.

If so, then the only thing that will get you out of lower back pain is to fix your hips—not to keep banging away on the lower back.

All the time I hear stories like, "I've had lower back pain for 12 years. I've had injections. I've had surgery. I get the latest and greatest treatments for my lower back."

And I say, "How do you know the problem is your low back?"

"Well, that's where I feel the pain."

If you told your doctor, "Hey, my left shoulder is tingling and I'm out of breath." and your doctor says, "Let's check your lungs and your left shoulder and get you out of here."

Would you think that was correct?

Just maybe there is something else going on. Maybe the pain is a symptom of something else. But with back pain you're convinced it's your lower back because that's what hurts.

I can't tell you how much it offends me when people go in to a doctor with lower back pain and they leave the doctor's office with a diagnosis of low back pain. That trained monkey in Thailand could have told you that—for a quarter!

That's why we do a full head-to-toe analysis of you, because your lower back pain and your loss of distance could both be problems that originate from your ankles, knees, hips or even from your neck.

We need to zoom in to the point where we can offer the correct diagnosis and the correct treatment.

The Trained Monkey Was Trained By Insurance Companies

Health insurance in this country only allows a doctor to treat the area of complaint, which means a lot of doctors—not chiropractic doctors, possibly—have been carefully trained to be the monkey.

They can't treat other areas of the body and still bill insurance for it. If they do it could mean legal trouble for them. So they treat the area you complain about. They might numb it, which works temporarily, but they won't chase down the cause.

The Lower Back

The lower back is the most commonly injured area of the body during the golf swing. It's also the most unreliable source of power. How about that? The most unreliable source of power. Unfortunately, it's the most commonly relied upon and overused source of power in the golf swing.

Let's go back to anatomy. The hips are meant to rotate right and left. If you think about golf, that's pretty much what we do, right? We rotate right and left.

The low back, meanwhile, is really meant to bend forward and lean back. The problem is that golf is a rotational sport, right? So we don't want to be just bending forward and back.

If we put that rotation, under power, into the low back instead of the hips, we crush small bones of the spine up against other small bones. There's your aching back.

The other problem is that there are some very sensitive structures in the low back. Nobody wants a disc bulge, right? And there's some tiny little ligaments and tendons that can get overstretched or even torn in the golf swing. That's a very common way of injuring your low back. Anatomically, it's just not designed to take the beating of a swing.

The hip doesn't have any of those very sensitive structures, whereas the low back has a lot of things that are very sensitive to pain and pressure. So you can use the heck out of your hips and feel fine, but your low back is not built for that type of use.

When you overuse it, you first become uncomfortable. You'll be sitting in the clubhouse after a round with your back barking and you go to get up after a round of drinks with your buddies and your back starts freezing. You hobble out to the car, get in and just can't find a comfortable position. As you drive home you wonder if golf is really the sport for you.

When you learn to swing with your hips, that big bone structure and huge muscle structure can take a beating, so you finish that round, and after an hour you stand up and say, "Hey, who wants to go and walk another 18?"

Watch the players on the PGA, watch their low back in their backswing. It moves very little, whereas their hips are turning quite a lot.

The Thoracic Spine

The part of the spine from the base of your neck to the top of your low back is called the thoracic spine. It's the part of the spine that has ribs connected to it. The word thoracic in medicine means "pertaining to the chest." So follow your ribs around from your chest to the middle of your back and you have found your thoracic spine.

This is also the part of the spine that tightens up when you are sitting in front of a computer for long hours of working, waiting to play golf.

In golf, this area is responsible for quite a bit of the turn, far more than people think. Now if you don't know how to say "thoracic," you probably haven't even considered stretching or strengthening it and you certainly haven't considered using it in your swing. I assure you, doing so will produce a much more consistent swing. In fact, we see many people whose low backs hurt because this area does not move enough.

The great thing about the thoracic spine is, despite how it may appear, it actually has a lot of room to rotate. There are 12 segments in it—12 individual bony segments. And a little bit of rotation occurs with each of these segments. This results in a lot of turn above the waist.

This is where a golfer's shoulder turn comes from. It's not your shoulders turning, it's actually your thoracic spine rotating. The ribs allow it to move in a circular direction.

Your ribcage/thoracic spine should contribute to 50 percent of your turn. The other 50 percent should come from the hips.

If your thoracic spine is too tight, then all of the rotation occurs in the few vertebrae of the low back. That puts a great deal of strain on those tiny muscles and ligaments, as opposed to letting that force be distributed over the entire spine.

We see that players with tight thoracic spines not only lack distance, but are very inconsistent. By doing the proper identifying, addressing and treating of the thoracic spine, we can help improve your consistency.

Most golfers are unaware of this. It seems to most that the ribcage is a fairly fixed/stiff structure not a rotational machine.

Shoulder pain in golf, as well as elbow or low back pain, usually traces back to the thoracic spine. If your thoracic spine doesn't move because you've spent too many hours slumped over your steering wheel or computer keyboard, loosening it up will make such a dramatic difference.

You'll notice in PGA players that the area between their shoulder blades is usually very flat their swing. When you have that very smooth curve there or flat area, it produces an easy, gentle rotational swing, and it's incredibly rewarding.

I think that's the swing that everybody wants. When the thoracic area is tight, you get some rotation in your backswing and through impact. The tightness there locks up and can cause you to slice the ball or lay your club face open, or maybe make you stand up out of posture.

Those things are distance-killers. You want to have that long, smooth, easy swing that gets you a lot of yardage and a low score.

How Your Feet, Ankles and Knees Might Be Mucking Up Your Swing Too

After we address the hips, thoracic spine and low back, we must address the feet, ankles and knees. These parts are often overlooked because most people don't sense tightness or pain there, yet they are.

Golfers don't typically look down at their feet and think they are a major contributor to the success of a golf swing when, in fact, we know they are.

Feet

First off, these two structures need to create a very stable base for you, because without one, you can't produce good distance. Imagine trying to stand on an ice rink in regular tennis shoes and hit a golf ball.

You'd be all over the place! So we need to make sure that your feet, with help from the ankles and knees, produce a strong, stable foundation from which you hit the hell out of the ball.

Your feet should be stiff enough to transmit force into the earth. You'd be shocked at how much force is actually pushing down during the golf swing. On a pressure plate it almost looks like somebody is jumping to produce that movement.

We also need the feet to be flexible enough to contour to what they are standing on. On a tee box you have a nice flat piece of grass, right? But many shots will be off angles—in the bunker, uphill, downhill etc. So we need your feet to conform to the surfaces.

Also, something I've noticed in some of the best players in the world is that their feet give them a lot of information about the slope of a green and the contours and breaks of the shot. So your feet can become very good as sensory organs.

Ankles

The ankles are a very mobile joint, or should be. They should bend forward, back, rotate left and right, rotate in and out. They help pivot and get your feet to conform to the different surfaces and the different angles.

Do you want to know how important your ankles are to your swing? Imagine trying to play a round of golf in a pair of really stiff ski boots. Most people don't realize how much their ankles contribute to the swing, but if you had ski boots going half way up your calves, your swing would be thrown way off.

Well, why is that? It turns out that your ankles need to move quite a bit to produce a nice smooth stroke. When you have an Achilles tendon injury, or maybe a tight calf or you sprained your ankle a few times in the past, it causes you to stand up out of posture and come down into the golf swing.

It's this wall of inflexibility that causes you to stand up—and send the ball all over the place. If you are a good enough player to make up for it at the last second, you're going to have to give up some distance.

You have to make sure those ankles are moving well.

A Patient's Success Story

One of my clients is in his late 60s and in great shape. A longtime golfer, he had a slice he couldn't get rid of. He worked with three different local pros, two of which were featured on Golf Digest's Top 100 list. But he just couldn't get away from this mean slice.

He was otherwise a very good player. He would compensate for the slice by hanging left, which is problematic because you just don't know where it's going to land.

We took him through a head-to-toe analysis and found that his left ankle had no movement in it whatsoever. It was just unbelievably tight! So I talked to him about his left ankle and it turns out that he has been trying to get rid of the slice for the last four years. He said he used to play much better, but now he has this slice which he can't seem to get rid of.

He said that four-and-a-half years ago he was moving and tripped coming down the stairs with a box, spraining his ankle and fracturing one of the bones. He went through rehab and the ankle was fine now, he said—never had any more problems with it. I asked him if he had any pain.

He said no, never.

He asked me, skeptically, if I thought the two things were related. To me it was clear that this was a big problem. To him it was no issue at all – *because it didn't hurt.*

We designed a treatment plan to loosen up his left ankle, which went really well. About four weeks later he came in and he said, "You are not going to believe this! I played golf Friday and Sunday and only had one slice off the tee!"

Here he'd dumped thousands of dollars into lessons with very good instructors but he didn't address that physical limitation. No instructor in the world could have gotten him to hit well.

Knees

Everybody knows when you hit the golf ball you should have a nice soft bend in your knees. You need to be able to move and flex. Knees also help you get down to retrieve your ball out of the cup, if it finally does make it there.

But most people don't realize there's actually a bit of rotation that goes on at your knee during your golf swing. You don't want a lot because that might injure your meniscus, but we do need a little.

Golfers who have had surgeries on their knees, or had a knee replaced, will benefit from getting those knees flexible.

In golf we call this tibial rotation. I've seen where we add maybe five degrees of tibial rotation and that resulted in 30 degrees of improved rotation of the whole golf swing.

A Patient's Success Story

I had another client whose instructor kept telling him, "You've got to follow through!" The goal was to produce a really nice fade. But he told us it was really tough for him to come through on the left side.

He was a very good player and was trying everything he could to achieve that follow through. We did a head-to-toe analysis and found out that he'd had ACL surgery when he was in college. He was 32 when we got our hands on him.

The surgery had limited rotation in the tibia, which makes it really tough to get all the way around to that left side. This diagnosis allowed us to tailor a specific plan for him. When he completed our treatment program, his swing dramatically improved.

How Your Shoulders, Elbows and Wrists Can Ruin an Otherwise Great Swing

We've talked about where you develop power (hips) and where you produce turn (thoracic spine) and the foundation of your swing. Now we've got to address the upper body, because that's what's actually holding the golf club! The upper body connects that golf club with the rest of your body and it's a very common to find physical flaws there. You may have heard of "golfer's elbow," for example.

So let's examine the shoulders, elbows and wrists.

Shoulders

We see quite a few players who complain of shoulders that have been tight for a lot of years, usually from slumping over a desk. Well, the first thing these patients need to know is that the cause of their shoulder injury was not their shoulder. It's likely their thoracic spine. In my clinic, nobody is allowed to leave with a diagnosis of a shoulder injury without the thoracic spine being addressed. If you go to see somebody who addresses your shoulder without looking at your thoracic, they're not a shoulder specialist and you need to move on.

Your shoulder has to produce a lot of external and internal rotation as your body comes through the golf swing. It's how you're able to get the face of the club to hit the ball squarely. So we want to make sure your shoulder is in good shape.

A lot of people get pain in the front of their lead shoulder during their backswing and at the front of their trail shoulder in the follow through or downswing.

The reason is your acromioclavicular (AC) joint can get a little irritated in golf. The AC is where your collarbone grabs onto your shoulder at the clavicle (a nerdy word for collarbone).

If you don't have that full range of motion in the shoulder, your club face may be a little too open or a little too closed. You may be sculling it. If you can't get the face of that club to squarely hit the ball, your distance will suffer. So, your shoulder can cause a big restriction to your distance as well. That's not uncommon.

Your shoulders need to be flexible. But on many occasions I've seen people who caused themselves a rotator-cuff injury because of the stretches they were doing to make that shoulder more flexible. They were not only the wrong stretches, but those shoulders didn't necessarily need to be stretched in the first place. It was likely the thoracic spine that's needed the work.

Elbows

Your elbows need to hinge up and down but they really shouldn't be moving sideways. If your shoulders and thoracic spine aren't rotating in the right direction, when you impact the earth, there's a lot of sideways force to the elbow.

That sideways force can tear up the inside of your elbow. And a torn ligament requires a long rehab, which prevents you from playing any golf at all.

Wrists

Your wrists are made up of multiple small bones, about the size of dice that make up a lot of the movement. The complex nature of the wrist helps you move your hands in a very fine manner to create exactly the swing you want. If you think about this in a baseball pitcher, the wrist is what allows them to throw a slider or a knuckleball or a fast ball.

Your wrists also allow you to hold strong for a real long drive and then soften up to create a finesse shot. Well, that flexibility in the wrists needs to be there. You have to make sure that every one of those bones is moving well.

If you don't, or your wrist is pinched and creates pain, that is one of the biggest power killers I've seen.

Chapter Four: How Your Short Game Suffers Along With You

Most of the time when you look in golf magazines and golf books, the thing that's being addressed the most is the long game (off the tee and your fairway iron). A lot of time it's the short game—from wedge play to putting—that gives golfers the most trouble. When I interview golfers before their analysis, they probably spend a third of the time complaining about that. When I ask how their back feels while putting, they look surprised and ask, "How did you know it hurts?"

Why Your Lower Back Aches During Putting

Well, if you've been overusing your lower back with every swing because your hips don't move or your ankles are tight, by the time you get to the green you are going to have an inflamed lower back. Your discs may be a little angry and injured, and some of those ligaments may be strained or sprained.

Also, when you set up with these shorter clubs, such as your wedges and putter, you have to bend over a little bit more to get the proper alignment.

At this point, you should be supporting the weight of your trunk with your hip muscles. But what I see a lot of the time, especially in the older working population, are golfers who support everything with their back.

We want to make sure that golfers adopt the correct posture because when you bend over and don't use your hips your lower back will complain.

I've had golfers tell me that they can't putt for more than 10 minutes without an ache.

These people are really in a tough spot because they've got that ache in their lower back and this pain won't go away - even with something that seems as simple as putting.

So the trick to getting rid of that pain is to line up the correct way and to bend over the correct way—making sure to use the hips.

When you use your hips you learn to engage your glute muscles, which are also the muscles that produce most of your distance. Now, miraculously, in seconds your lower back pain goes away or you just don't feel it anymore. It's not that you fixed it (yet), it's that you are asking a different set of muscles to work.

In the short game we want your lower body to be very, very quiet. The best short game players in the world use their upper body a whole lot more, their wrist, elbows, shoulders and hands. Whereas the best distance hitters in the world use their hips more.

A lot of people think during their short game is when their back is strained and their lower back is injured. Their body reacts by not wanting to move those lower segments at all and that unconscious tension can go quite a way up the spine. When your body locks down the back in a reaction to pain, all you have to hit with is your arms and maybe a little shoulder turn. That makes for a very inconsistent shot.

If I gave you a football, asked you to throw it through an open window and I back you up by 20 yards – you'd probably get it through the window after about three shots, right? What if I sit you in a lawn chair and I don't let you use your hips at all. Now, you'd be all over the place.

You'd be up, you'd be high, right, and low, whatever. Well, why is that? Because the ability to use and incorporate your hips and the weight shift they allow really increases your consistency.

The same thing is true in golf. We know you are not going to use your hips in the short game, because we said the best players don't want to use their hips, but everything above that should be used to create that perfect shot. When it's not, you're all over the place.

This would be a guy that takes his approach three feet short and the next one he's 10 feet long and the next one he's way right and he's all over the map. We say the only thing worse than being short is being inconsistent as well. If you are inconsistent, you may be swatting at the ball with your arms without producing a smooth swing.

The short game isn't as likely to produce injuries, but it could aggravate what's already there and your short game could fall apart due to other injuries.

A Note About Putting …

When a golfer has pain bending over to putt, I might ask, "Do you have pain in your lower back in life or during other parts of golf?" If their answer is no, give it a month.

That person, if they have pain when they're putting, will have pain within a month, guaranteed. It tells me that their glutes are totally shut down and can't even support them bent over a putter. That's a ticking time bomb.

Also, if at one point you were consistent and now you're totally inconsistent and you can't seem to figure out why, I would look for a physical cause. This is very, very, common.

There is likely a physical cause pulling your swing apart and you can't figure out why. You don't feel pain, necessarily, but there is something wrong. Like I said earlier, if you played in ski boots you wouldn't say that you were in pain, you just can't move correctly and it messes up your swing.

I have a proprietary set of protocols I use to help people golf better. They consist of analyzing your vision and the way that you see shapes and how you line up to a ball. This allows us to dramatically lower people's scores.

Our putting analysis is one of things I am most proud of. I've had patients reduce their score by three strokes within one week! This is mostly achieved by putting in correction that knocks out the three-putts. If you can get those three-putts down to two-putts, that's an easy way to reduce your score.

Chapter Five: The Quest for *Your* Perfect Golf Swing

An amazing thing that I've learned is that there's a commonality between all of the greatest hitters in the world, no matter what their swings look like.

It doesn't matter if you're Jim Furyk or Luke Donald (who pretty much have opposite swings). There's a similar quality among them.

That commonality is what's called the kinematic sequence.

The best players have very similar timing and sequence of their swing. That means if we look at the top of the back swing transitioning into the down swing, those players always activate their bodies in a certain order.

That order is:

1) Hips
2) Pelvis
3) Trunk
4) Shoulders
5) Arms
6) Hands

It's kind of like a bullwhip. The thick part of your body goes first, and as it goes it accelerates until finally the tip moves last—the thin part. This produces the most power and fewest injuries. When the order of the kinematic sequence gets messed up or even reversed, we can accurately predict an issue.

And by that I mean there's going to be a problem with your swing, a loss of distance and/or an injury.

Now this sounds kind of crazy, but let me explain this another way. If I asked you to throw a tennis ball, I know your shoulders are going to turn, then your arm is going to extend, your elbow is going to straighten and, finally, your wrist is going to snap. You know instinctively that that's what going to get that ball to go the furthest.

If I took you out of order and said, "Hey, now I want you to throw this ball the same way, except this time instead of your wrist going last, I want it to move first." We would have exactly the same muscles, same joints, same ball - everything will be exactly the same – except for the order of those two things. We know that ball would go nowhere. You just wouldn't have the power. And if I asked you to do it over and over again, there's a really good chance that something would start hurting. That something might be your shoulder, or your back, but whatever it is would slow things down further.

If you swing a golf club in the correct order you're going to feel a really easy swing and watch that ball go flying down the fairway. And you'll think, "Wow! I didn't even hit it that hard."

That's right, you didn't have to hit it that hard because you used the correct order. Sometimes, when your order is off, you can try as hard as you want and you just can't get back in line.

We can help make sure that your use of the kinematic sequence is preserved because, again, no matter what your swing looks like, there has to be the correct order of joints moving to create an optimal ball flight and distance. This really wasn't discovered until the use of three-dimensional analysis. That's when consistencies were found among all those top players.

Imagine mastering this sequence and becoming one of those golfers who effortlessly smack the living hell out of the ball.

I recommend that every player gets checked out on 3-D annually to make sure that their kinematic sequence is preserved. This can also detect potential injuries. Or let's say your lower back is sore. Is it safe for you to play in that tournament coming up? Are you just going to have a sore back afterwards or is this an incredibly dangerous proposition?

One of the ways we can tell is if you have pain but your kinematic sequence is preserved. If that's the case you're probably just going to end up with a sore back. It's not ideal because you are still in pain, but at least it's just a sore back.

What we really want to look for is, do you have pain and is your sequence off? If so, you are, possibly permanently, damaging both your body and your swing. And those a big problems to overcome mentally and physically. You're programming your brain to have a different swing.

3-D Analysis

If you're serious about your golf game, I recommend that you get a 3-D analysis done. It will reveal so much useful information about your swing. Most of the bigger golf shops around town, such as Golfsmith, will have a 3-D system. We also work with the pros over at the nearby GolfTec.

A decent 3-D analysis puts a minimum of three sensors on your body, usually at your hips, your thorax and your wrists. Those three sensors record how you move up, down, left, right, forward and backward. It will display what you do on screen with a little avatar, which shows us what joints are moving which way. We have certain parameters to use to analyze if you are doing damage during your swing. Properly analyzed, the 3-D tells us a lot.

There are optical versions of this system, too, where little reflective balls are put on you. The MAT system and a company called GEARS use this method. You're filmed and as those reflective balls move with your body.

These are other systems that measure your movements in different ways—from electromagnetic fields to inertial sensors—in order to create a 3-D representation. But they all produce the same information, so we don't really care which one you get.

That being said, I do have a preference: the K-Vest 6D system, which uses a kinematic vest.

It's also a good idea to get a 3-D analysis when you are swinging at your best. That way we can outline what body positions you're in when you hit the ball well. So I could say, "We know you hit the ball really great when you have 17 degrees of forward lean and your knees are bent at 21 degrees."

And later, if you get to the point where your swing is absolutely falling apart, we can identify objectively what angles put you in the best shape for your style of swing. We can get you back there really easily.

Mobile Joints Connected to Stable Segments

There was a conversation that occurred between two of the smartest people I know. One was a guy named Mike Boyle, who a lot of people think is the number-one strength coach in the world, and another guy by the name of Gray Cook, who may be the best physical therapist in the world.

One night, they were exchanging ideas as to how they look at the body. They came up something astounding in its simplicity.

They noticed that the human body is a series of mobile joints connected to a series of stable segments. Also, there is an alternating pattern of mobile, stable, mobile, stable, mobile, stable. Now when that pattern gets reversed, problems arise. You get pain, decreased performance, etc.

I share this with all of my clients, and they all love how much it helps them understand their body.

Let's look at this closer. Starting with the foot, we want that foot to be a stable segment. Each foot has three arches, and we know it has them in order to maintain stability. Same reason why engineers put arches in a bridge. We want to make sure that foot stability is maintained.

The next joint up is the ankle, and this needs to be mobile. The ankle needs to move forward, back, rotate in, rotate out, and tilt side to side.

The next joint is the knee, and we know that has to be nice and stable. It can bend forward and back, but we do not want the knee to twist or dive in or dive out. A lot of NFL careers have been ended by a knee that's moved in the wrong direction.

That takes us to the hip, which needs to be a very mobile joint. In fact, it moves in six directions, making it one of the most mobile joints in the body.

The next series of joints is the pelvis and lumbar spine (lower back). Sometimes this is referred to as the core. Most of have read or heard by now how important a strong, stable core is.

The thoracic spine is next, and it should be very mobile. It should help you rotate a lot. It should flex forward and back and tilt side to side.

The next joint up is where your shoulder blade meets your back—the scapulothoracic junction. That should be a very strong joint (but is often compromised).

That stable shoulder joint is where we transmit power from our upper body to our trunk when hitting a golf ball.

That takes us out to the shoulder, or glenohumeral joint. This should be the most mobile joint in your body.

And this alternative pattern continues: Elbows should be stable, wrists should be mobile, hands should be stable.

If everything is working properly, you have the ability to hit the ball very far with the desired ball flight. Anytime that order gets reversed, there are problems. A common thing I see with patients is that they have reversed this order, leaving their hips trying to be stable. They are not moving; they are stiff and inflexible. This creates a chain reaction: The lower back becomes mobile instead of stable, and the thoracic spine is stable instead of mobile.

When that reversal happens, what happens to the lower back? It's now gone from mobile to stable and ends up getting torn apart. We see discs bulge and herniate. We see even fractures occur.

All this because the body is searching for a way to move and the hips and thoracic spine are not properly responding.

In a perfect world you could wake up in the morning and consult your body to find out if your stable segments are stable and your mobile segments are mobile. If all is well, you go play. If something is out of order, then you'd fix it before you go play.

If you wanted to fix any issue when you're in pain, you would need to check that the mobile joints were mobile, that every stable segment was stable, and that there were no asymmetries in either side. This is actually done when we analyze someone — which is one of the reasons we spend so much time with our clients.

This concept, by the way, is the basis that we use to correct the kinematic sequence.

Chapter Six: Putting It All Together

There's a lot that goes into the golf swing. We know there's the kinematic sequence, which sits on the foundation of the body being a collection of stable sections and mobile segments.

When somebody comes in and says their back hurts or that their swing is falling apart, we know that they want that to change. The result they are after is usually pretty obvious.

But we don't know what they're starting with. The mistake that a lot of golfers make is they go to see somebody for help but they get into that trained monkey situation where they say, "My back hurts." and the doctor just focuses on their back.

The only way we can really see how you are doing is to check you from head to toe, and that's a much taller order. It also takes a lot of time. If you go into an office and the doctor takes five minutes to assess you, odds are he's examining the place you said hurts, and that's not going to help you create the swing you want. That's also not going to help you get better. You need more than that, and you should demand more than that.

Our first step in our approach is a test that identifies whether the mobile parts are mobile and the stable parts stable. Through experience, through trial and error, through frustration and through suffering my own back injury, I found a proven formula that ensures success. It is called the Selective

Functional Movement Assessment (SFMA). It's a series of tests that we take you through. Based on your results, the assessment may comprise upwards of 164 specific tests.

It's possible that there are multiple things going wrong, and we keep testing until we've identified every problem. Then we take those issues and make a long list of the mobile things that are not mobile enough and the things that need to be more stable and we prioritize them. Based on those results, we start treating you.

That first part takes a long time, and if we are also going to film you and incorporate 3-D analysis, it's going to be even more time.

But don't forget, we are talking about golf here. We're not talking about someone's desire to sit on the couch without pain. We're talking about can you bomb a drive on the 18th tee box, not have pain, finish a round and decide to play the next day. That's our goal, and if sounds lofty, good!

We don't want to just make it so you can be without pain at home, that's not how life is lived.

After the testing and results analysis, we determine the most effective treatment for you, and that starts with eliminating your highest-ranked problem.

For example, if I know that your ankle is tight and doesn't move properly, I have a five-step ankle protocol that we will use to make that vital joint mobile again. If your hip is not mobile, we have our proven six-step formula to get your hip to be more flexible.

That's how we treat each issue we find. After treatment, we need to figure out how to keep that problem from coming back. I struggled with that part for a long time. I would see people in the office and they'd come back a month later with the same issue. So, I searched out some of the finest home flexibility programs and home strengthening programs in order to help our clients, not just get out of pain, but stay out of pain.

When you execute these exercises perfectly and do them consistently, you will see increased driving distance and decreased back pain. You will also produce a much more consistent golf swing—one with power and that feels good. That's a pretty big reward.

Chapter Seven: Get Tough

Once we've successfully addressed your pain, we begin to teach your body to move properly. We want it to move the way it was meant to move, allowing you to create a long, straight ball flight. Again, just imagine how it will feel when your drive bombs past your playing partners and goes 25 yards farther than before.

One of the most important aspects to build on at this point is what we call "durability." I use this word to describe the basic amount of required flexibility and strength.

Balancing both of these creates a body that can put up with quite a bit of golf—even a few missed shots and improper moves, yet be resilient enough to play another round the next day.

We work with quite a few college golfers, and we see how incredibly resilient they are in playing tournaments that are 36 holes on the first day and bouncing back to play 18 the next day. And, by the way, they walk the whole time! So obviously durability becomes a big factor.

In recreational golfers, durability is the ability to play an even score on the front and back nine. I hear golfers telling me that they need "a few holes" to get going, and then they "drag through" the final two or three to finish the round. This only leaves a few holes for them to make some decent shots. That's no way to play—or to live!

So we have each of our players develop an individual systematic approach to durability. In our gym programs at Anthem

Fitness, the stretches and exercises are tailored specifically to each player. You really have to see them in person to appreciate them, so here I will only talk about the most common restrictors on durability and how to combat them.

This lesson starts with the best tactics I know of for improving your durability: daily maintenance, driving-range prep and post-round recovery. It's a regimen to help ensure that every piece of your body is turned on and working properly.

Every Tour pro I know of has a morning routine to check up on things and to make sure that every muscle works in your swing. If something isn't working, your swing has to change, and we can't have that.

So we will start with daily maintenance, which include stretches, exercises and routines a golfer implements every single day. These are the biggest factors in their success.

It does take time and effort. But we have a client in her 60s and she has executed her daily maintenance better than anyone I know. Her reward is a dramatically changed swing and lower scores. She couldn't be happier. She will tell you that it's the little things every day that make the biggest difference.

My best recipe for success on a daily basis is the following combination, which takes less than 20 minutes:

- Full-body foam rolling.
- Hip, thoracic spine, shoulder, lat and ankle flexibility stretches.
- Isometric exercises (preferably the series developed by Dr. Tom House).
- Rolling patterns.
- Crawling.

Let's start at the beginning.

Foam Rolling

A lot of people label foam rolling as a flexibility drill. I think of it more as a morning massage. It helps you remember every part of your body by giving it a little wake-up stimulation.

Plus, the moving around that you have to do to position yourself on the foam roller is a great little core warm-up. Most of the positions are like planks in their nature. You can see this in the pictures below.

One quick note here: A tendency I see in a lot of people is they aggressively roll areas that are painful. I have NEVER seen this work out in a positive way. When an area is in pain, it is typically inflamed. Rolling that area on a foam roller may cause an unwanted increase in inflammation.

On each area, I would spend 15-30 seconds and gently roll to wake everything up. This isn't a race. It's time to get familiar with your body.

(If you would like a video of this routine, text the word "FOAM" to 702-728-4788.)

First, start with the back of your hips.

Hamstrings

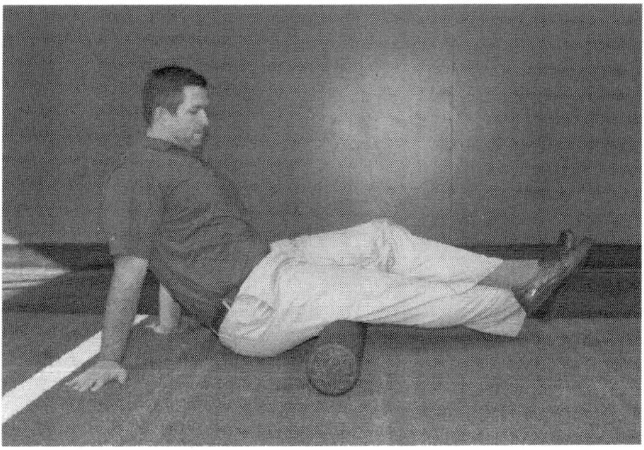

Calves

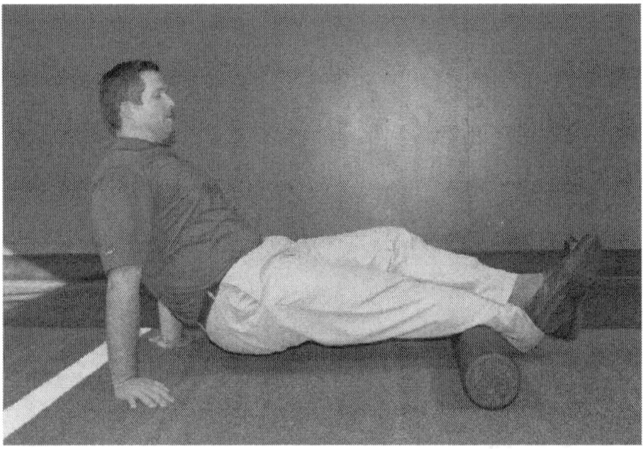

Then transition to your spine, being careful not to roll too low, as it can injure your low back.

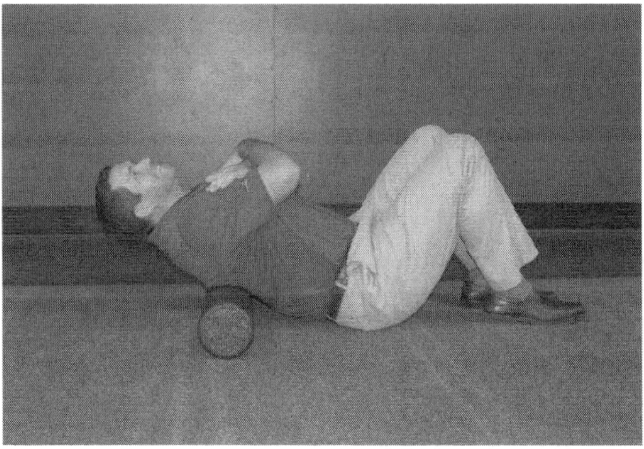

Turn your chest 45 degrees and get your lats—very important for golf.

Now flip over and get your quads, rolling them with a bent knee.

Now, roll the inside of your thighs, the adductors. Watch out, this can be pretty uncomfortable.

Finally, finish with the IT band.

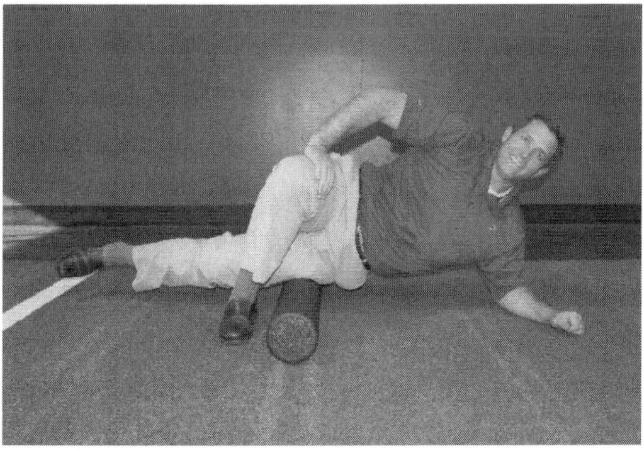

Stretches

This series of stretches should also be a part of your morning routine. Going back to the mobility/stability model, the safest "one size fits all" approach is to stretch the areas we know should be mobile. I've included my favorites here as well.

(If you would like a video demonstration of these stretches, text the word "MORNING" to 702-728-4788.)

This first stretch is called windshield wipers. It's for your hips.

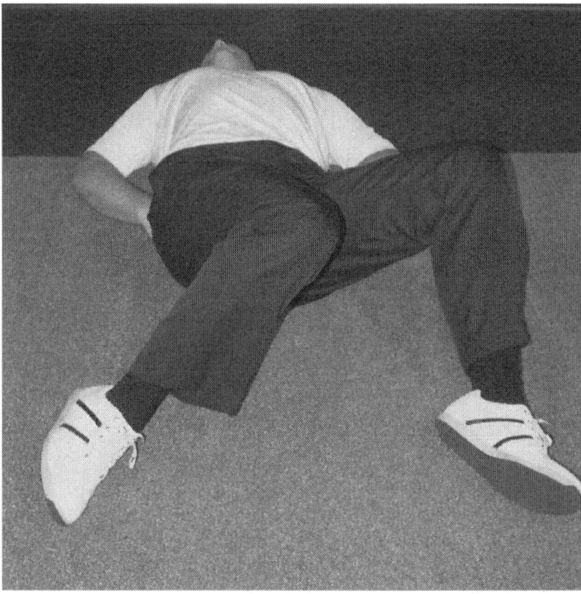

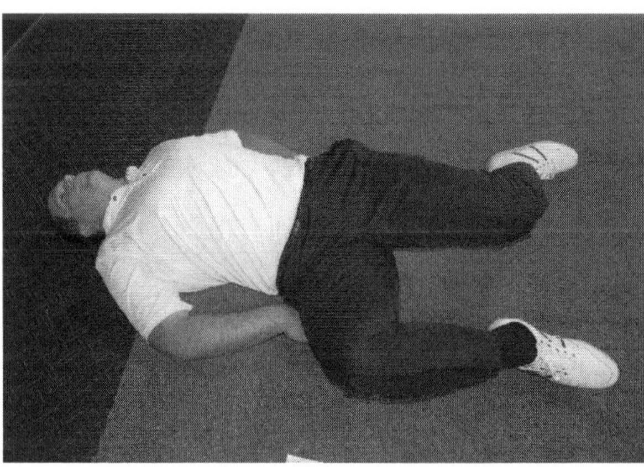

Brettzel

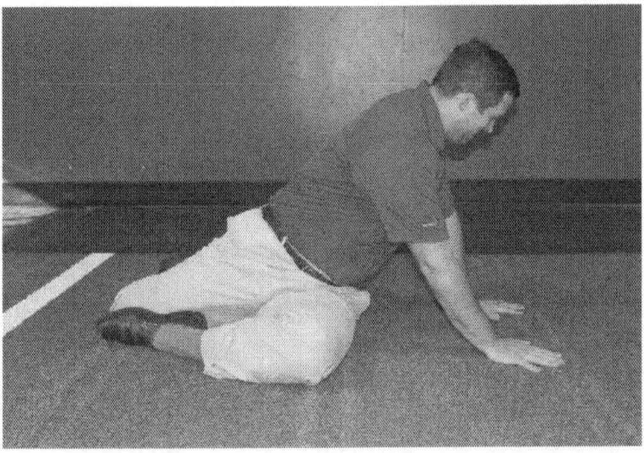

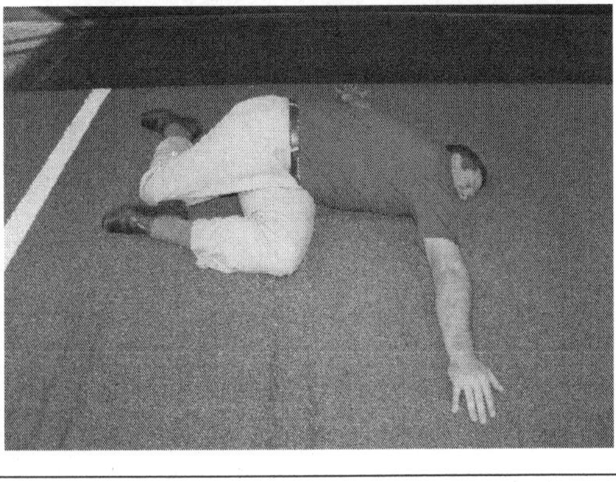

These are for the Thoracic spine. They're called Open Books.

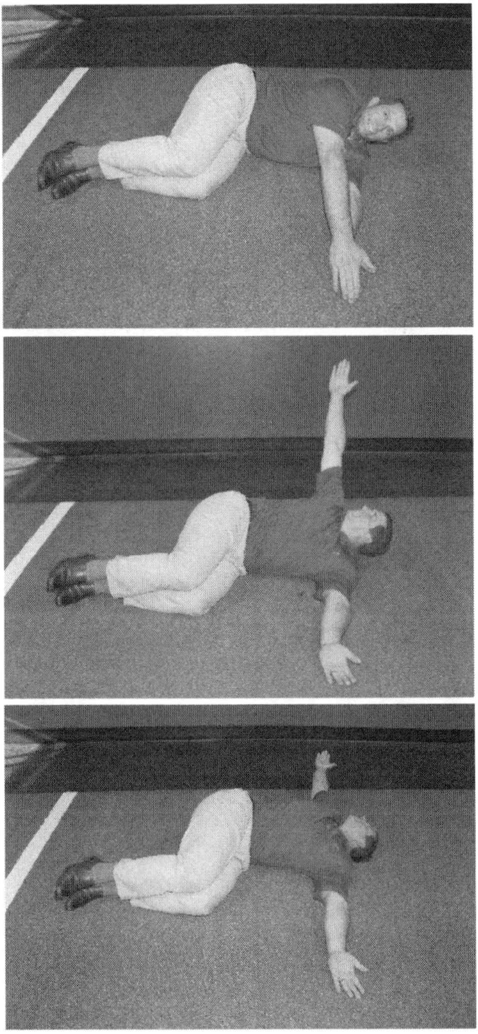

Q-ped Reachbacks

Shoulders: Shoulder Sweeps

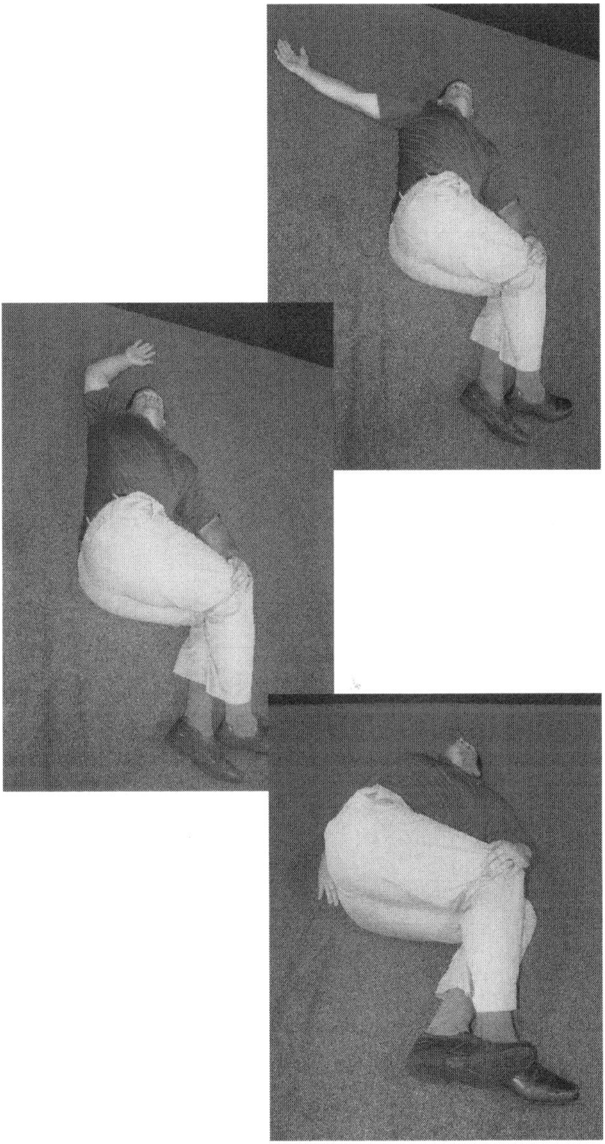

Wall Angels

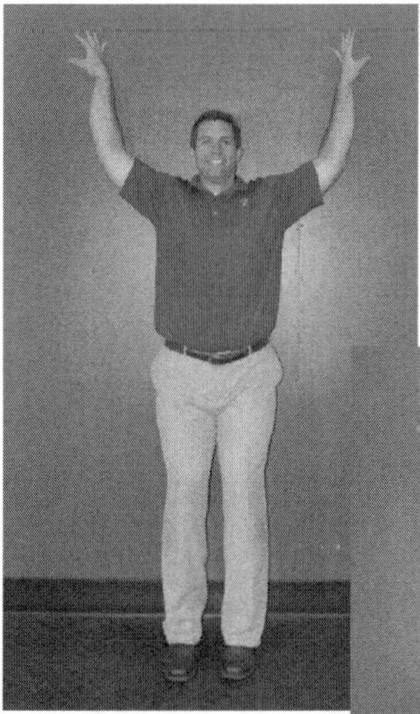

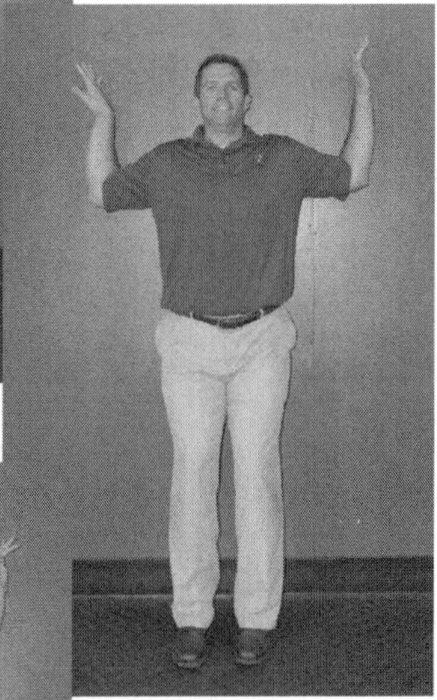

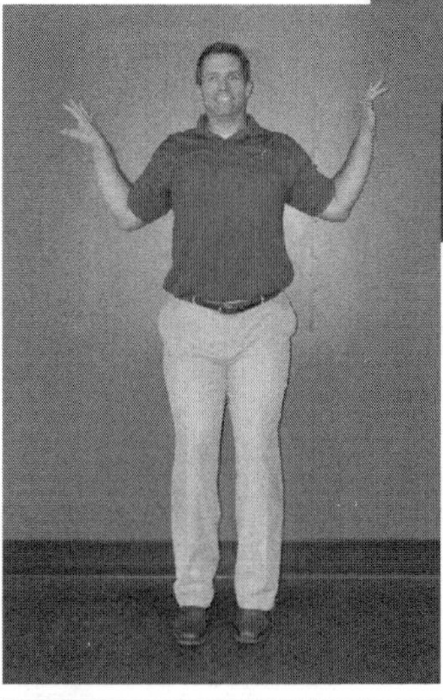

This one is for your lats:

Ice Skater Stretch

Ankles:"21 Game"

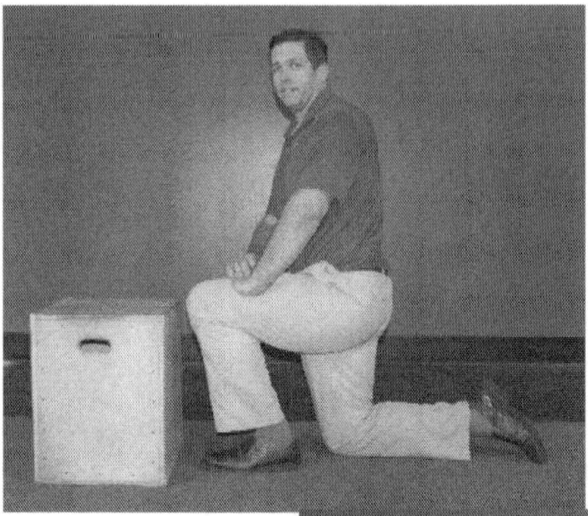

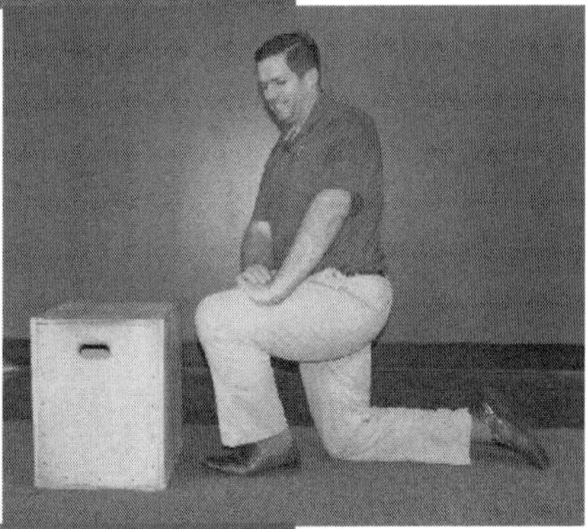

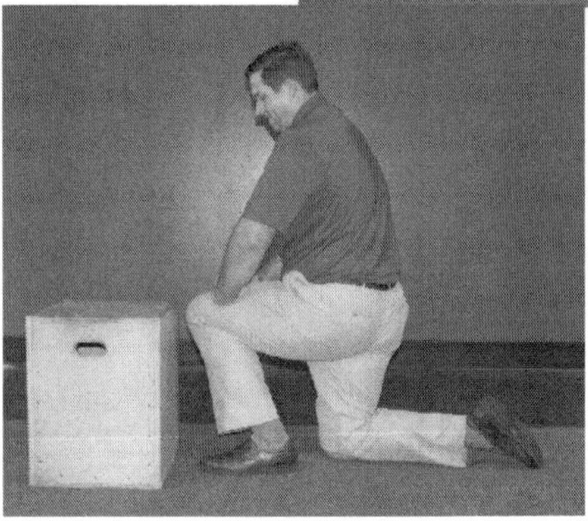

Isometric Exercises:

I have found that isometric exercises are a fantastic way to ensure your body is turned on and ready to work. Isometric exercises don't require any equipment, and they also turn on the muscle fibers before movement. This is a very big deal. I don't want your warm-up to be some dangerous, explosive movements! I learned these exercises directly from Dr. Tom House. He has a whole routine - lying down, with a chair, using a wall, and standing. For our purposes, we just tart with the lying down drills.

(PS- If you want a real challenge, learn all 4 routines- and perform them every day for 30 days. I'm sure you'll be dramatically improved in your movement! Dr. House is in his 60's, and I've seen him crush College athletes into a heap of sweat, while he is calmly joking in his dry sense of humor.)

(To see a video of this routine, text the word "HOUSE" to 702-728-4788)

Figure 4 Over

Figure 4 Under

Rolling Patterns:

Of all the "exercises" I have used, taught, or seen in the last few years, none has made as enormous an impact on my patients as these Rolling Patterns.

They work like a giant "Reset" button for the body and brain. If you have kids, you'll recognize these as the first real movement a baby does. The day they roll over is a BIG day, because they are starting to integrate their bodies and movement patterns.

Before this day, they can maybe move an arm, or their head, yet haven't "put it all together" yet. So rolling just helps integrate all the parts and pieces into a useable unit. This is usually much harder than most think it will be. I invite you to try all 8 patterns.

To communicate their power, I'll share this: At the President's Cup Tournament when it was held at Muirfield Village Country Club, both the American and the European teams could be seen using rolling patterns in their warm-ups. Shouldn't you?

(For a video demo of these, text the word "ROLLING" to 702-728-4788.)

Right Arm Prone to Supine

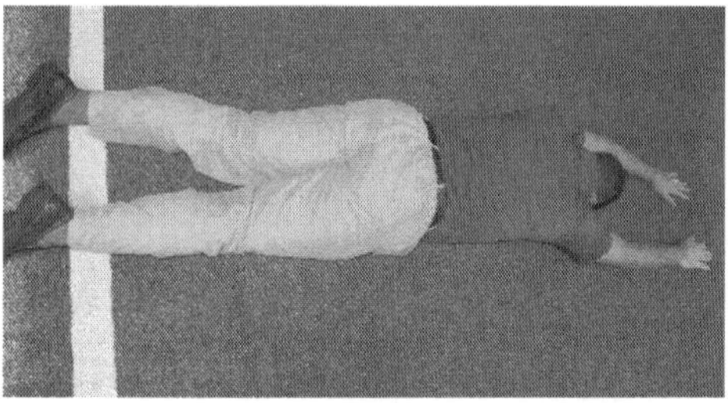

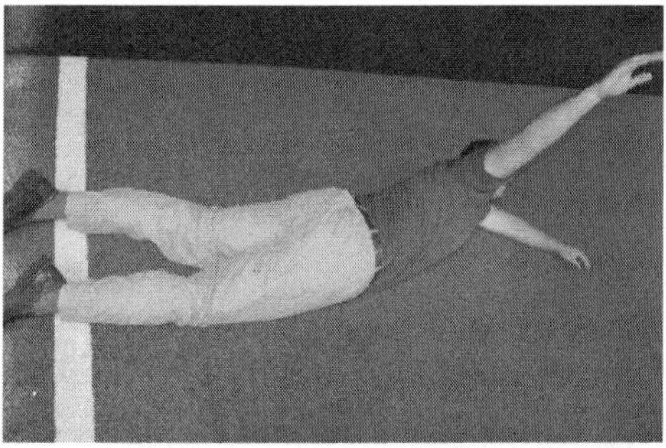

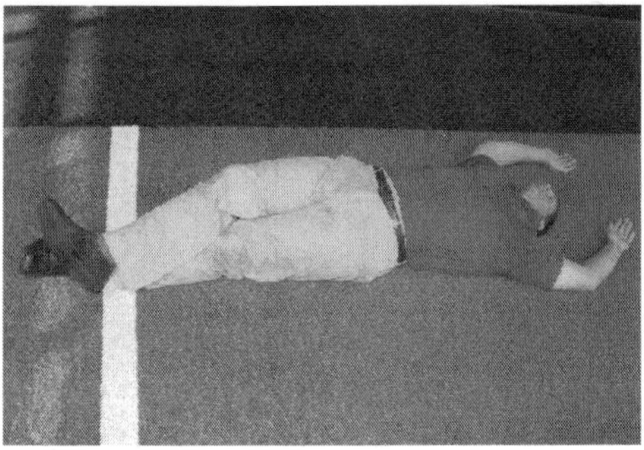

Do the same leading with the left arm.

Right Leg Prone to Supine

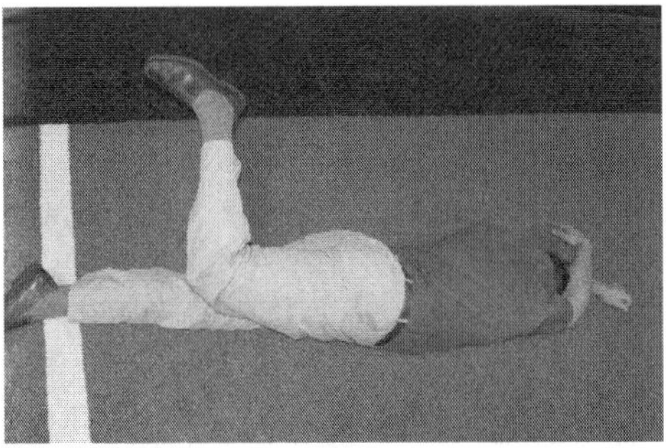

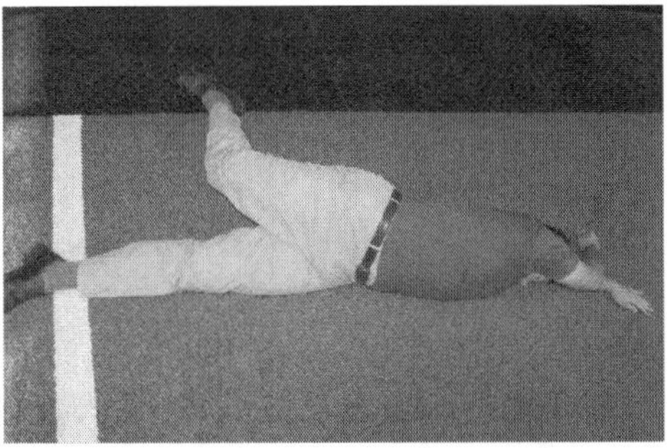

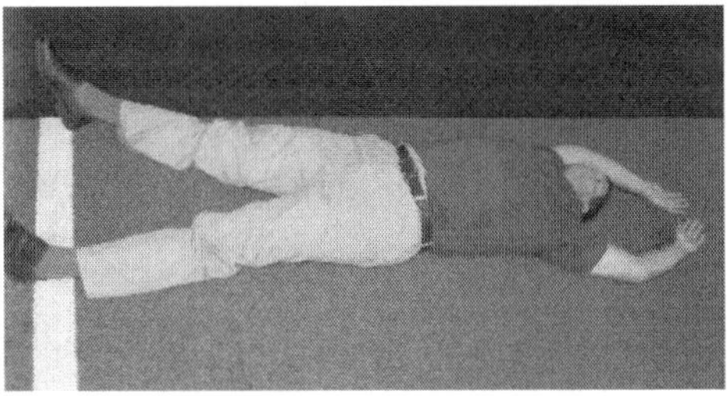

Do the same leading with the left leg.

Right Arm Supine to Prone

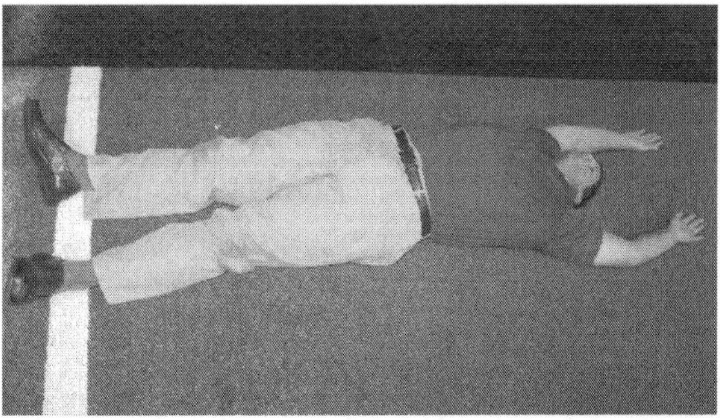

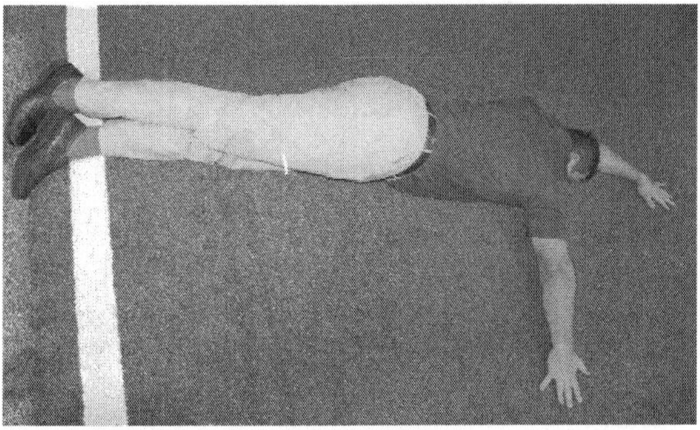

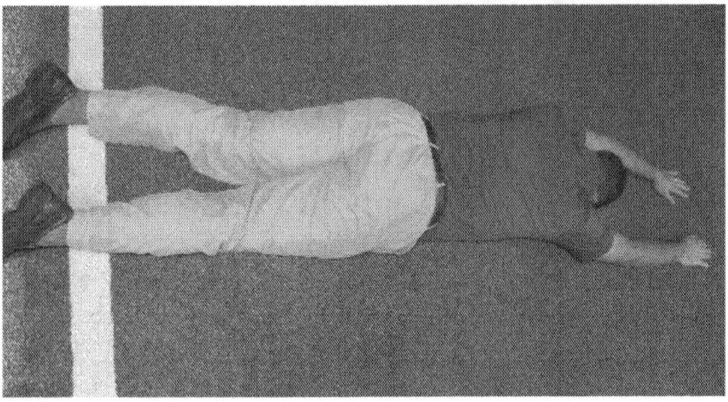

Do the same leading with the left arm.

Right Leg Supine to Prone

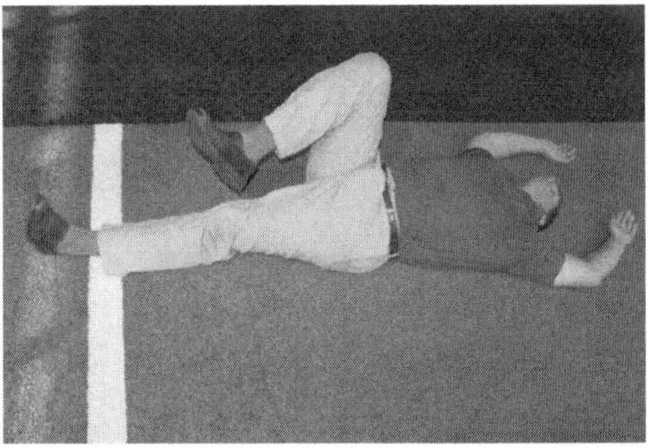

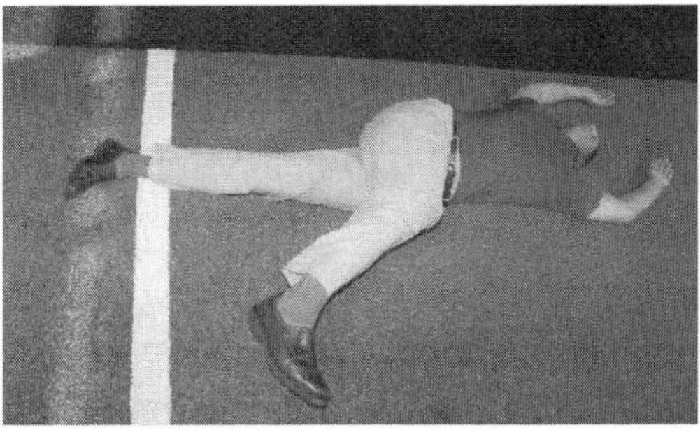

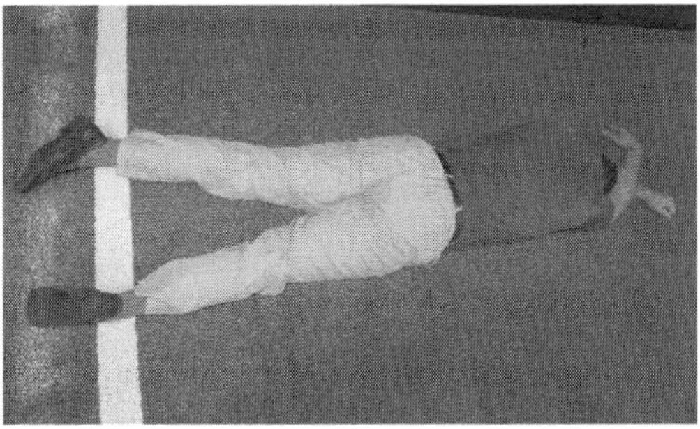

Do the same leading with the left leg.

Crawling

I love crawling. It is a fantastic way to warm up the body and get everything moving. Just like rolling, it's a great way to integrate everything. Plus, it's WAY harder than you assume! I think it's a great way to warm up with no equipment needed.

You see, the crawling requires a strong, stable core, and helps turn on the muscle needed to gain serious distance and take the dang cover off the ball. As soon as you crawl, you'll see how much work has to occur in your core. And when that strength connects to the driver — WATCH OUT — 20 yards is nothing!

Here are my favorite 4 crawls to perform every morning:

(To see a video demo of these, text the word "CRAWL" to 702-728-4788.)

Bear Crawl Forward

Bear Crawl Backward

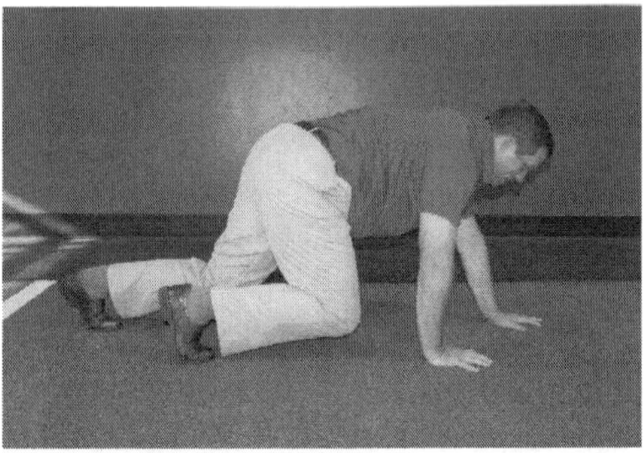

Side Plank Crawl Right

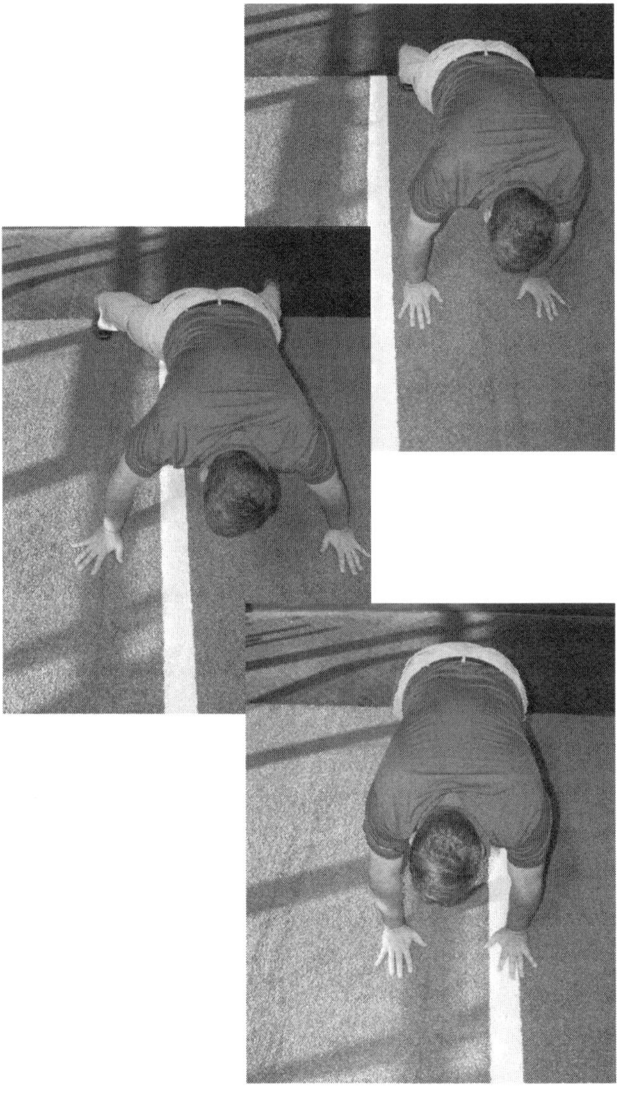

Do the same crawl left.

If you perform this routine every morning I feel strongly that you will become very durable. And if you want to get a routine that is specific just to YOU, then you should participate in our full Evaluation or even our Full Experience. You'll leave both of those with a set of exercises and stretches that are specifically designed for YOU and your swing. They will help you gain even more distance!

Conclusion

We have talked about many of the factors that affect your golf swing. I hope I have illustrated the most common limitations.

To conclude, I'll leave you with the number-one way I believe you can lower your handicap and make the progress you are looking for on the golf course. And that is to address your body's physical limitations.

Earlier, you learned that having the option and ability to move well in multiple directions opens up so many possibilities out on the golf course. And be sure to visualize what it will be like to be the last player to hit the ball. Think about how rewarding it will be to drive to all of your second shots and being the last to go. Imagine being 20 yards ahead of your best playing buddy.

To achieve that — and I believe you CAN achieve it quickly — you must address any of the swing limitations we spoke of — whether it's C-Posture or a nasty Slide. We covered some simple ways to change these at home through foam rolling, stretching, and performing the same specific exercises that we see used on the PGA Tour.

If you are still struggling to gain any distance after working on those drills on your own, we would love to help you out.

In fact, if you've read this far in the book, I know you are hungry for distance and that you're driven. We love working with motivated players like yourself. I want to offer you an opportunity to find out exactly what is holding you back. And it all starts with our customized, personalized, one-on-one PGA Tour-level assessment. You need that high-level assessment to tell what's needed.

This is a two-hour intensive analysis where we check each and every joint, and score your ability to produce power in your swing. We also measure the most critical data on your ball speed and club-head speed. If you are interested in a 3-D analysis, our talented coaches will take you through an elite analysis as well.

Every day, we have golfers going through a one-on-one, two-hour complete assessment for $350. Since you have read this far, I know you are different than most players. You are truly interested in getting better, and because of that, I'd like to offer you a $50 discount on our evaluation.

This two-hour process will be the best two hours you have ever dedicated to your golf game! It will take you to the next level, helping to increase your driving distance and split the fairway.

To set up your appointment, just call our staff at 702-558-2151 and mention this book. They will know what to schedule you for.

Again, picture how it will feel to out-drive your playing partners — pretty incredible I bet.

Call to set up an appointment today and get started NOW.

Yours in health,

Dr. Josh Satterlee, DC

Index

About the Author

Dr. Josh Satterlee is a Chiropractic Physician, Strength Coach, and a nationally recognized presenter on the subject of injuries facing golfers and other athletes. He owns and operates his clinic, Bio-Mechanics of Las Vegas, in Henderson, Nevada, where he treats golfers at different levels of the game every day. Attached to his clinic is a integrated functional training facility, Anthem Fitness, where his team works to help golfers gain driving distance and feel better every day. When he is not working with clients, Dr. Satterlee is a husband and father of 2 boys, Adam and Owen, who are already picking up the game of golf at a young age.

If you are interested in booking Dr. Satterlee for a speaking engagement or a workshop, contact his office at (702) 558-2151.

29514157R00080

Made in the USA
Middletown, DE
22 February 2016